AND YET HELD

AND YET HELD

POEMS

T. DE LOS REYES

BULL★CITY
PRESS
DURHAM, NC

And Yet Held

Library of Congress Cataloging-in-Publication Data

Names: De Los Reyes, T., author.
Title: And yet held : poems / T. De Los Reyes.
Description: Durham : Bull City Press, 2023.
Identifiers: LCCN 2023032858 |
ISBN 9781949344448 (paperback)
Subjects: LCGFT: Poetry.
Classification: LCC PR9550.9.D3925 2023 |
DDC 821--dc23/eng/20230814
LC record available at https://lccn.loc.gov/2023032858

Published in the United States of America
Book design by Spock and Associates
Cover art: "Forget Me Not" by Alexxander Dovelin

Published by BULL CITY PRESS
1217 Odyssey Drive
Durham, NC 27713
www.BullCityPress.com

I want to love you longer, say it again,
I want to love you longer

—ARACELIS GIRMAY
from "I Am Not Ready to Die Yet"

CONTENTS

For T.

DEBRIS

Ask the prophets and they'll say the universe
quivers when something tender happens
that they did not intend: a little girl learning
to tap dance over a small puddle, a stranger
opening the door for another stranger, pieces
of coriander warming the taste of broth. Debris
falls with each shuddering breath, and the fissures
of our days murmur their thanks for every good
thing we are allowed to have. The grasshopper
on the balcony railing. Jeans I can finally wear
again. Forgotten salsa at the back of the fridge.
Of course the unknown scares me sometimes
and I cry when my grandfather visits me
in my dreams. But today ice cubes melted slowly
in my coffee cup, and you looked at me from
across the room in a way that made me feel held.
Oh, how I am but skin fragmented by touch, from
which a little flower blooms amidst all the wreckage.
And, having been found, waits to be kissed.

THUMB

Have you been eating the donuts,
you asked suspiciously, hips leaning
on the doorjamb as if you've always
belonged there. I turned to say yes
and was suddenly struck by every
little thing I have failed to tell you.
How your voice is a red thread tied
to my little finger, calling me to come
back after being out in the deep dark.
How often I say I'm cold so you can be
the big spoon when I just really needed
to be held, and how I didn't really like
pineapples all that much before but now
they are just the sweetest thing. That
whenever I check if you've eaten I am
actually saying I love you. That I don't
mind washing your dirty underwear, that
I have an urge to kiss your eyelids from
time to time, and oh, I've been staring
for so long with my mouth open you are
standing before me now wiping sugar
crumbs off my lips. Here is your thumb;
it is saying, *I know, you doofus, I know.*

BOWSPRIT

Cold water. Feeling the world sway
as he steps forward on the prow

asking *You want the moon*? As if
he has the power to give me

the impossible. As if by asking I am
finally unmasked and found clinging

wildly to air hanging by my heavy
bones at the end of a bowsprit.

The deep wave comes closer and
I cry *please* and *please* and *please*:

a tender transaction between skin
and skin. Salt on my lips and a hymn.

DRIFT COMPATIBLE

Loose monsters on earth
and it's down to the two of us
to do something about it. Would you
be the left brain or the right and how
prepared are you to finally see what has
been living inside my skull. Would you
step into the gleaming armour ready
to be soldered together for good
or ill. Would you embrace what
unfolds in my imagination and
even further still: how far are you
willing to go to kill the savage
coming to the surface. My knees
tremble the way your hands shook
the first time you touched my face.
I will let you in but I cannot promise
that you will remain the same
the same way you cannot wholly
guarantee my safety in the labyrinth
inside your head. Here, now, as we
roam in each other's memory upon
memory, hold fast. I see a golden
collar you put around my neck I see
the sputtering bus you get on I see you
burrowing under a blanket I see myself
reading a book I see you washing the dishes

I see your teeth descending upon my skin
and then we move heavily as a colossal
fist through water trying to save the world
yes I have to save it and I will save it
because your mouth
your mouth

LEAF

Today you were emptying
your pockets and out falls

a memory from the fire tree
that watched us kiss. Never

mind the wrappers of candy
you promised not to eat

anymore or that key you
swore you put back in our

hiding place. Might be I seldom
write about mysterious things

instead choosing moons and
fried eggs and your skin. Look

at you now gently holding
an unsuspecting leaf unaware

I was looking. When a little smile
lifts the corner of your mouth

who needs secrets

THE SHAPE OF RAPTURE

1

We were nameless except for the number seven.
Seven years of seeing each other grow into young
women for seven hours of the day all seven days
of the week with seven subjects taught by Sisters
in habits. She loved the smell of my hair. I loved
that she could find anything to love about me.
The centres of her palms were so soft, as were
her eyes. Her letters were carefully folded like
tiny shirt pockets. *Dear Seven*, was how they always
started. One time she saw me across the room
and *Seven!* carried over the distance. My name was
an endless echo and in the darkness I found my way.

2

Way too naïve at sixteen, he believed the height
of sophistication was a teddy bear. I found I was not
immune to his charms. I, too, was silly in my ministrations:
I put his photos on the cover of my Trapper Keeper,
an announcement that *I am loved.* Today, Monday:
I am loved. Today, Tuesday: *I am loved.* And so on.
We were too young to come up with our own words.
Bless those who came before us and described how
hair is a waterfall lightly meeting a lover's nape.
Bless those who touched the pad of their thumb
upon sweet lips, bless those who knew the texture
of whispers. I learned to yearn through strangers.

3

Strangers sitting around a circle decided to play a game of who would you fuck but there was no spinning bottle. The power was out and we were all dying with thirst and desire. We threw down names like currency and it's the story of my life, isn't it, of being found tender yet strange, as if a painter's brush made a wrong stroke on the canvas. I'm what some would call an acquired taste: too much heat, too much weight. Didn't think someone would utter my name. Then his mouth opened. In my mind a man in a suit handed me a life-sized cheque, and the papers published their latest: "Fool Wins Lottery, Wrecks Her Life."

4

Life of the party, I told him I liked to lick my fingers.
I was at that age when I felt I could be dangerous.
I said, if we were alone we would already be in bed.
His mouth went dry. He fell silent for hours, and I
could hear everything he was not saying, his words
landing like invisible confetti: *kiss* and *kiss* and *kiss*.
We sat in the dark listening to each other breathe and
I was a fool, sign me up for another cheque. No one
tells you when a word suddenly turns from a promise
to an infringement. Look up *tomorrow* look up *soon*
look up *before you know it* and you'll find me on my knees
grappling around in the dark, hoping there is still time.

5

Time to get down to business as you toe off your shoes.
How much do you want me, you ask, as if a challenge.
I want to peel off your skin. Climb into your ribcage
where your heart is. Every day we get to love each other
in a world that does not want us I praise our bodies.
We can do that, your voice muffled between my thighs.
Can't we? How come you don't scare easily how come
you don't think I'm creepy as fuck how come
you don't laugh at my granny panties how come
and come and come you whisper, all lips and tongue.
I howl with your mouth around me. Please—I want
to ache again and again. We can do that. Can't we?

VALSE SENTIMENTALE

and then you
and my hand
and the parting crowd

and hyacinths
and dreaming trees
and feast of clouds

and spinning
and coming back
and laughter

and roaring sea
and fading sky
and stillness

and stars flee
and pulses thrum
and stutter

and breathless plea
and then your lips
and me

FOREST FIRE

It is bad enough that somewhere in our lives
something is always breaking. On forsaken days

all I can be is a bystander watching the world
go awry. It takes so little for a sigh to ignite.

Someone lights a match and the wind understands
what it is to persist. The woods hiss with the heat,

roots gripping the scalp of the earth. If mercy exists
your hand will be on my cheek wiping soot away.

Ashes crumble on my skin, held but for a moment
before vanishing. What I mean when I say hunger

is your open mouth between my thighs and a promise
that we will both burn. Can it get any worse, this life

and everything in it. Can you hold me when I am
unbearable and especially then. What I mean when

I say thirst is your eyes drinking me in, telling me
you'll dig through bones and cinders just to be here,

wherever here is.

UMBRA

Didn't I have too many fears to reasonably
survive in this world. Wasn't I scared of dying
suddenly or slowly, whichever way: by car
collision, accidental fires, earthquakes, a wave
of flood, by electrocution because of the flood,
or by simply forgetting how to breathe. Look,
I am terror struck by the monster living under
my skin, and of loving that monster regardless.
And hadn't you draped your shadow around
my shoulders saying, I will hold you, I will hold
you now and always, I will hold you and I will
yes, I will

TURNING IN EARLY

because I said I'd write. Can't remember
how many times I've told people that and
then simply ended up on the couch reading
or burrowing under the blanket to sleep.

Now my pen charts a course between thought
and the empty page wondering how to tell you
of the faults in the world I can't protect you from
or how a body can become an excavation of loss.

In from a stroll sans an umbrella, you come
up to me, showing a bug bite on your arm,
your skin warm and isn't this tenderness,
how someone loves me enough to show

a bug bite. I'm turning in early because I said
I'd write. Here is the wild beast knocking about
my chest. It wants to say the mark on your skin
reminds me of a distant star and may I touch it

with my lips. The night is heavy with what we
cannot name, including the hitch in your breath
upon bowing my head. Need I abandon my one
task to describe our life. Need I let words fail.

HARD HEART

This is for the girl with the hard heart
who said it's a mire out there and there

is no way she would get spattered with
the mud of living. This is for the girl

who carefully put on her boots before
going out the door and tried her best

to play hopscotch with everything
she wanted to avoid: a neighbour

who secretly fixed the fire exit door
because all the banging kept her up

and the shop owner who called a cab
when she got lost somewhere in town

and that one time she hurried to a public
bathroom when she got her period and

a stranger slipped her a pad under the stall
and that time she gasped when she saw a dog

and it turned to lick her hand and oh how
about when he told her she was beautiful

the first time and then the second time and
last night for the six hundred millionth time

yes this is for the girl who refused to be bamboozled
with the small gestures of this sodden world: my love,

look at all this tenderness which threads through
our life, which is given freely, which is ours

ABOUT GRAVITY

I hold your hand across
the yawning dimensions

as the thread of time is
woven into our being

here. The way dust is.
The way love is.

The way our bodies
yearn toward the centre

of the earth as if a bamboo
tree bending down for a kiss.

Always leaning, always
falling. And yet held.

RAVENOUS

I am five hundred years older
than you, I said while breaking
open the soft flesh of honey
oranges. Surely the sweetness

fades the more these holy bulbs
become exposed to air and palms
and tongues, surely there are other
reasons for crossing the universe

to be here. He tells me: I am always
ravenous for your waiting mouth.
What I would not give to have you
turn your head when I say your name

CATCH

Catch in your voice when you say my name,
catch in your breath as you empty yourself of yourself.

Catching my hand as I put my palm over your telltale heart,
catching my gaze before your eyes slide down my skin.

Gasp from your lips as the lush universe
starts to settle beneath your ribs,

grasping the back of my thighs and hips,
as I, too, submit to the surface.

Wisps of your hair feather my face.
I place ellipses on your neck.

Whispers of worship perish before they land.
The *and* of your hand.

MONSTERS

1

We begin with a desire to devour.
I am a citizen of want, my body
a country of bruises from your teeth.

I am happy to pay in sweetness
as long as it is you who takes
my lips. Once, upon coming

to a clearing, we hurriedly shed
our clothes, feral things whose
vocabulary knew no waiting.

I am happy to be here before you,
palms up, wanting and being wanted.
Once more, and once again.

2

Someone once took me to bed
and wanted to fuck in the dark.
I was a body and yet not a body.

Someone mistook me for not being
me when they read my words but forgot
my name. Where do I hide my shame.

I was a body and almost somebody.
We damn well know: to be brown is
to always be guilty of being brown.

3

Who wouldn't want this,
hands around my throat,
hands that cup my breasts,
hands that grip my hips.

Let me whisper confessions
to the shadows on your skin:
When I see your open mouth

I hear the selfsame howl from
deep in my womb: I am your
leviathan among the woods.

4

This is what it means to shiver
beneath someone's gaze,
your possession teaching me
the length of my spine.

Who wouldn't want you,
telling me you're home
and safe from standing
before an invisible firing line.

In the subway, at the pharmacy,
at the grocery, in the park:
when have we ever known
what it means to be apart.

No one can stop me
from holding your hand,
not even the demons that
corrupt their heart.

5

Would that there were a menagerie
inside your warm body for every
living thing that you might have been:

the tenderness of a butterfly, perhaps,
or the startling softness of a bird.
A sweet longan.

6

How do you conjure
an ever after. I wish
nothing more than
to follow where this leads.

Our bodies unfurl from the core
and everything hurts

while we stand in line at the bank,
or when we walk across the street
to get to our door.

When they call you names
or when they call mine,
I will always want you
whispering in my ear:
Why not right here.

7

Oh, husk that houses who I am!
Almond eyes, thick thighs,

and every ember that has
settled on my dark skin.

I want your wildness—
and damn the rest of them.

HOW DO YOU SAY X IN FRENCH

I asked my teacher once, watching
her lips closely as she enunciated
words I would eventually forget.

Cheese, I requested, and coffee,
and what time the train leaves.
Sunny weather and how to go to
the market. How to turn right. How

to turn left. Also: ten stamps, please,
and I have a stomachache. They all
just rolled off her tongue, oui, très beau.

I studied for weeks but life happened.
Things you don't get to use that often
become consigned to oblivion. And yet.

J'adore, I whispered, one day, as I watched
you take out the laundry. I felt foolish
speaking in a language that isn't yours

or even mine, as if my brain blitzed and
reached for some random thing rattling
about. How do you say I am a wild thing

and now utterly yours, how do you say
excuse me, sir, but I have fallen madly.
Laughing, you take my hand, and lift

my wrist to your lips, my pulse skittish,
a creature suddenly found and about to
bolt. *Like this.* Exactement. Exactement.

TEETH

You have the hunger of a thousand skeletons
begging to be surrounded by flesh again.

Your fist is a locket that holds my name, and
beneath the desperate wings of your eyelashes

I am learning about surrender.

Let me bare my neck for your waiting mouth:
if you mark me it is because I asked to be loved.

SIMPLEST LOVE

He asks me for my dress size
and I hesitate. He looks at me,
knowing the answer, but asks
anyway, letting the rest of our
lives stretch in those seconds.
I'm a simple guy, I remember
him saying when we first met.
If I say it I mean it, that's the
gist of it. Yes, I could feel every
wall I've ever built tremble and
it's not about the dress, is it,
it's this body you love, the one
you hold every night. Rooted
out and disarmed, how could
I let this happen. He takes my
face in his hands. Not found
out, he whispers, but found.

WITNESS

You are spinning round
and round, your whole body
committing to the rapturous
display. There is no music,
and people passing by give
a wide berth yet can't help
glancing back. I am almost
an intruder, as you turn and
turn on your toes, arms out
as if wanting to welcome
strangers home.

                    Whatever
the rest of the night brings,
the rest of my life, too, in this
wretched world, let me have
this for a little while. Please
let me have you, beguiling
and dancing, as close to the
divine as you can possibly
get, as if we can't be hurt,
no matter how much we try.

BODEGA

When I walked around the ladies' section
unaware my dress was open all the way

to my belly button, I didn't even feel
the cold. I was running my fingers

through a silk shirt while they played
holiday songs. In September. Imagine.

And when I grabbed groceries from a stranger
and carried them two whole blocks to the car

thinking he was my father, I could only remember
how heavy the bags were, and who buys two dozen

cans of fruit cocktail anyway in one go. Imagine.
What is outrageous. I was in the elevator and

an elderly lady walked in and said hello. Naturally
I said hello back and when the doors opened

she held her phone to her ear and walked away
from me forever. All of these I now unearth

from the undercroft of memory. You were hurting
and I asked if you wanted to be held. You said yes

in a voice I was hearing for the first time. I wanted
to shake loose the bodega for words that would mean

this is our life and I am yours and you will never
be alone again. So I told you about a pleated collar.

Eight hundred twenty-five grams of cherries in syrup.
My surprised face reflected on the chrome doors.

Listen: in this world I have been unbuttoned. Yet
in the same life you are laughing until you are crying

which means mission accomplished. This time
I am certain I am outrageously loved. Imagine.

BECAUSE I WAS HUNGRY

you find me barefoot rooting around
the fridge past midnight. *Not the nachos,*

I hear you say, and I turn around startled
out of my wits. It's like when I was running

after the bus thinking it's over, I'm late for
the nth time and the boss is going to fire me.

Then she called in sick last minute, thank you,
universe. Or when it was my turn to cook in

home economics class and I forgot the spring
onions. My sister came bursting in, out of breath,

then threw a battered brown bag at me before
rushing out, saving my life. And what about when

I heard what I thought were gunshots outside and
it was only fireworks. Or when I thought I lost my

passport in Singapore but it was in my inner jacket
pocket the whole time. What I mean is: here I am

with cheese on my lips. And you are smiling and
shaking your head and saying, *come to bed, come.*

NOCTURNE

The ocean-sized silence
begs for language where
lovers speak with gestures.
I wear your hand like a collar
around my neck and in the dark
I am found, my heart skipping
like stone across the clear water.
Quick now, before it sinks,
before I disappear again, please
kiss me. I feel your lips tremble
as if you are about to drink from
something holy. And isn't it. Isn't it.

GARGANTUAN

It was a disaster on a gargantuan scale. I fell in love
with wonderment and have become as transparent
as a bougainvillea leaf. Here: sesame seeds embedded
in a cookie. Here: the soft centre of a sunflower. Here:

the tiniest mole on your earlobe you didn't even know
existed until I kissed it. I have nothing to offer the world.
Meanwhile moon crescents indent my pillow and outside
an old man with no teeth is selling pineapples. Who knows

if it's a pilgrimage of distance or years before I finally get
to myself. Who else have I allowed to hear the ridiculous
and faulty pendulum in my chest forming a rhythm of
shit shit shit shit shit. We carry within us everywhere

we have ever been: our bodies housing cities housing bodies.
I once stood breathless before a pagoda face-to-face with what
I can no longer deny. When I said I loved delirium I meant
your eyes. A cloud is a wound in an otherwise empty sky.

What if our memories have expiration dates and all the things
I feel are tickets flying around in a lottery machine. My childhood
is a city where tenderness was frowned upon, yet you are now
holding my body, whose shape is exactly what I need it to be.

I read the dregs at the bottom of my mug as if portents, as if
my ancestors' faces, as if pieces of Pangaea torn apart by
the earth's fissures. I call you my beloved in all the languages
residing in my throat, your name an ululation in every lifetime

we will ever be in. What is delight if not half of your collar still
turned up as you walk out the door, and wasn't it an occasion
to touch. If they cut me open they will find words etched
deeply on my bones: Brown. Awake. Aurora. Woman

wonderstruck at being found whole after the wreckage. Ah, self:
thank you for not further collapsing into a heap after the untimely
discovery of the rest of your life. Hasn't it always been what is fatal
and without pity. And hasn't it always been about love.

DELICATE

The pale lines on your skin are rivers
I would gladly bow to, tongue touching
your open fist, my chosen altar. I want

to cradle your taste in my mouth, the way
two animals gently nestle together in a dark
cave where it will always be warm: this thumb

I love, this forefinger I love, and this one, and
this one. Ah, my beloved. How do I describe
how it is to want. The more I try to dig around

language, the closer I am to knowing what words
lack. Come let us burrow into the soft earth as if
we are gifted hours upon hours that will never end.

I forgive the god who has made us luminous beings
merely passing through this lifetime: because here
is your palm, because my lips have touched it.

OLD FRACTURES

Woke up to the sound of church bells from a few blocks away.
Your arms wrapped around me like a cocoon I am loath to
part with. What is sacred, I asked you once, quite determined
to not get anywhere near it, afraid of ruining and being ruined.
This body you're holding a broken cup you let your lips touch
over and over. The faint toll a steady rhythm as I put my ear
against your chest. I nestle closer and from the distance I can
hear myself, the lone ringer pulling the rough rope, proclaiming:
GOOD MORNING! I LOVE YOU! GOOD MORNING!
I remember prayers you gave me. One as the sun rises: I am
not going to die today. One for the blooming moon: I am
grateful to be alive. If I am quite incoherent, please forgive me.
My heart has cracked open like a window, holy, holy, holy.

NYMPH

I was swimming in the warm light,
hair down to my back and finless.

May I stay like this, I asked, wanting
to be allowed this small kindness.

The tips of your fingers slowly traced
my brow. I felt as light as a cloud

on your palm. Bending down, you
whispered my name inside my mouth.

FIST

There are days when I am a fist, and that is all
there is, fingers nestled toward the centre.
Something frail brushes against it accidentally,
an eyelash perhaps, or breath from your lips
saying, *open, open.* I hesitate, knowing nothing
is there to surprise, no pearl hidden among
the days. Uncurling, I show you my naked palm.
Look, you say in delight, placing a small kiss.

PINEAPPLE

There will be a next time. That much
I can say. When I was young I feared

submerging my hands in the wet murk
of dishwater in the sink, afraid of what

I'd find down there. And I always ran
from my bedroom to the bathroom

when I needed to pee at night, refusing
to glance at shadows. I learned to fear

darkness, thinking it was a gift I would
not want. No one told me it was the last

thing that could hurt me in this damn
world. Today I watched your mouth close

around a slice of pineapple like a kiss. How
my pulse skittered, as if my fingers had grazed

the sharp edge of the knife underneath
the suds, as if a gigantic silhouette suddenly

had formed in the corner of the room. Oh
dearest child, how I wish I could tell you

the most devastating of all threats is
love. That it is fruit which will be our

greatest undoing. That the next time
the gathering gloom arrives, we will bear

the cavernous and unplumbed terror of not
wanting to die. Of finally wanting to live.

NEAR LIGHT

We watched the rocket slowly ascend
amidst a storm of clouds on a night
where nothing of note had happened
yet. It could have been just another
day except a giant engine left the earth
to find out what else exists apart from dust
and gas and how necessary a quest it is,
how terribly glorious to see every little
mortal thing fall away from view. Here is
what I know: your heart is a fist that holds
the galaxy. What I love about a ship going
to deep space is the proximity near light
and darkness and the reluctant decay of
days and years. When you kiss me I forget
my name. I forget myself. I recognise only
the skin and bones that house this body.
Permission to disturb the gods in slumber.
Permission to scatter, as if hundreds of fish
in the warm sea, as if an exploding star.

ACKNOWLEDGMENTS

My deepest gratitude to the editors of the following publications, where some of these poems first appeared in earlier versions:

Cordite Poetry Review: "Monsters"

Crazyhorse: "Fist"

Hobart After Dark: "The Shape of Rapture"

* * *

A whole universe of thanks to Gabrielle Calvocoressi, Mandana Chaffa, Aerie Em, Shira Erlichman, Al Filreis, Krysta Lee Frost, Annelyse Gelman, Jennifer Huang, Liesl Jobson, Itiola Jones, Robin Kello, Davy Knittle, John Minczeski, Jenny Molberg, Mira Moss, Bonnie Naradzay, Daye Phillippo, Richelle Sushil, and Lesley Valdes, whose kindness, generosity, and encouragement have nurtured my writing life and spirit;

Ross White, Noah Stetzer, Alana Dunn, and Bull City Press, whose belief and guidance provided an invaluable refuge for my poems;

Cheri, Sacha, Chinky, and my parents, whose presence profoundly transformed my journey as poet;

Pat Alampay, Myka Arnado, Raphael Atienza, Katherine Bandanwal, Kae Batiquin, Kit Diaz, Keet Geniza, Abigail Go, Sunny Katigbak, Karina Kim, Jilly Lanuza-Baltazar, Vittorio Milanes, Raymond Molina, Nel Mondoy, Yot Morales, Arianne Policarpio-Shi, Charmaine Que Pua, Susan Scheid, Emma Sedlak, Shirl Tin, Jack Young, and Maiky Zabella-Roxas, whose enduring friendship and unfailing celebration of my work have been a source of strength and shared joy;

And to Tevin—with tenderness and love

ABOUT THE AUTHOR

T. De Los Reyes is a Filipino poet and designer. She is the author of the chapbook *Woeman*, published by *Hawai'i Review*. A finalist for the 2021 Sappho Prize by *Palette Poetry*, her poems have appeared in *Birdcoat Quarterly*, *Crazyhorse*, *Hobart After Dark*, *Pleiades*, and *Split Lip Magazine*, among others. Her work revolves around womanhood, eros, and mapping the body—exploring geography vis-à-vis the question of identity as a person of color.

Past recognitions include Notable Manuscript for the 2016 Chapbook Prize by BOAAT Press and First Place in Filipino Poetry in the 2007 Maningning Miclat Poetry Awards. She was named a Fellow for Filipino Poetry in the 2006 Ateneo Institute of Literary Arts and Practices National Writers Workshop.

De Los Reyes is the founder and curator of *Read a Little Poetry*. She is the designer of *Nowruz Journal* and a mentor/community teaching assistant for Modern and Contemporary American Poetry (ModPo), a highly successful, massive open online course offered by the University of Pennsylvania, for the past decade.

She lives and writes in Manila, Philippines.

This book was published with assistance from the Fall 2022 Editing and Publishing class at the University of North Carolina at Chapel Hill. Contributing editors and designers were Megan Pramojaney and Jonay Sutton.